God Hears You

GOD HEARS YOU

compiled by Larry Richards

▣ ZondervanPublishingHouse

A Division of HarperCollinsPublishers

To: _Lilles_

*Prayer is one of your privileges as a
member of God's family.*

From: _Tom_

The Bible contains many prayers uttered by God's people. These prayers serve as models for us, helping us to express ourselves to the Lord.

*Scripture is also rich in promises that
give us a foretaste of God's answers
to our prayers.*

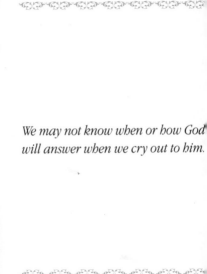

We may not know when or how God will answer when we cry out to him.

But we do know that he hears us, and that he will do what is good for us.

Your Prayer . . .

Rescue me, O LORD, from evil men;
protect me from men of violence.

Psalm 140:1

...God's Answer

Fear of man will prove to be a snare, but whoever trusts in the LORD is kept safe.

Proverbs 29:25

Your Prayer...

*Let the wicked fall into their own
nets, while I pass by in safety.*
Psalm 141:10

. . . God's Answer

The faithless will be fully repaid
for their ways, and the good man
rewarded for his.

Proverbs 14:14

Your Prayer...

Make us glad for as many days as you have afflicted us, for as many years as we have seen trouble.

Psalm 90:1

…God's Answer

I will repay you for the years the locusts have eaten.

Joel 2:25

Your Prayer...

Summon your power, O God; show us your strength, O God, as you have done before.

Psalm 68:2

...God's Answer

In the time of my favor I will answer you, and in the day of salvation I will help you.

Isaiah 49:8

Your Prayer...

According to your great compassion blot out my transgressions. Wash away all my iniquity and cleanse me from my sin.

Psalm 51:1

...God's Answer

As far as the east is from the west, so far has he removed our transgressions from us.

Psalm 103:12

Your Prayer . . .

*Do not bring your servant
into judgment, for no one living is
righteous before you.*

Psalm 143:2

...God's Answer

The LORD is gracious and compassionate, slow to anger and rich in love.

Psalm 145:8

Your Prayer . . .

I have been disciplined.
Restore me, and I will return.

Jeremiah 31:18

. . .God's Answer

*Make every effort to live in
peace with all men and to be holy;
without holiness no one will
see the Lord.*

Hebrews 12:14

Your Prayer...

Teach me knowledge and good judgment, for I believe in your commands.

Psalm 119:6(

...God's Answer

Now that you know these things,
you will be blessed if you do them.

Your Prayer . . .

I seek you with all my heart; do not let me stray from your commands.

Psalm 119:10

...God's Answer

*I will put my Spirit in you and move
you to follow my decrees.*
Ezekiel 36:27

Your Prayer...

Lord, listen! O Lord, forgive!
O Lord, hear and act! For your sake,
O my God, do not delay.
                                    Daniel 9:19

...God's Answer

I will heal their waywardness
and love them freely.

Your Prayer...

*Let the morning bring me word
of your unfailing love, for I have put
my trust in you.*

Psalm 143:

...God's Answer

I tell you the truth, until heaven and earth disappear, not the smallest letter, not the least stroke of a pen, will by any means disappear from the Law until everything is accomplished.
Matthew 5:18

Your Prayer...

Let the heads of those who surround me be covered with the trouble their lips have caused.

Psalm 140:

...God's Answer

I will punish the world for its evil,
the wicked for their sins.

Isaiah 13:11

Your Prayer...

Arise, LORD! Lift up your hand, O God.
Do not forget the helpless.

Psalm 10:1.

. . .God's Answer

*They will live securely, for then
is greatness will reach to the ends of
the earth. And he will be their peace.*

Micah 5:4-5a

Your Prayer...

I confess my iniquity;
I am troubled by my sin.

Psalm 38:1

. . .God's Answer

Return, faithless people;
I will cure you of backsliding.
                    Jeremiah 3:22

Your Prayer...

O righteous God, who searches minds and hearts, bring to an end the violence of the wicked and make the righteous secure.

Psalm 7:9

. . .God's Answer

*He will judge the world in
righteousness and the peoples
in his truth.*

Psalm 96:13

Your Prayer...

Teach me to do your will.

Psalm 143:10

. . God's Answer

I have set before you life and death,
blessings and curses. .
Now choose life,. . . love the LORD
your God, listen to his voice,
and hold fast to him. For the LORD
is your life.
Deuteronomy 30:19-20

Your Prayer . . .

Restore to me the joy of your salvation and grant me a willing spirit, to sustain me.

Psalm 51:1

...God's Answer

The LORD will establish you as his holy people, as he promised you on oath, if you keep the commands of the LORD your God and walk in his ways.

Deuteronomy 28:9

Your Prayer...

I am in pain and distress; may your salvation, O God, protect me.

Psalm 69:2

...God's Answer

Our God is a God who saves.

Psalm 68:20

Your Prayer . . .

Lead me, O Lord, in your righteousne.
because of my enemies –
make straight your way before me.
Psalm 5.

. . .God's Answer

Whoever lives by the truth
comes into the light.

John 3:21

Your Prayer...

*Do not be far from me,
for trouble is near and there is
no one to help.*

Psalm 22:

...God's Answer

I will be faithful and righteous to them as their God.

Zechariah 8:8

Your Prayer...

Remember not the sins of my yout
and my rebellious ways;
according to your love remember r
for you are good, O LORD.
Psalm 2

...God's Answer

If you repent, I will restore you
that you may serve me.

Jeremiah 15:19

Your Prayer . . .

Do not cast me away when I am old; do not forsake me when my strength is gone.

Psalm 71:

...God's Answer

They will still bear fruit in old age,
they will stay fresh and green,
proclaiming, "The Lord is upright."
Psalm 92:14-15

Your Prayer...

Teach us to number our days aright,
that we may gain a heart of wisdom.
Psalm 90:1.

...God's Answer

e faithful, even to the point of death,
and I will give you the crown of life.

Revelation 2:10

Your Prayer...

Turn to me and be gracious to me,
for I am lonely and afflicted.
Psalm 25:1

. . .God's Answer

I will rejoice in doing them good.
Jeremiah 32:41

Your Prayer...

*But may all who seek you rejoice
and be glad in you.*

Psalm 70:4

…God's Answer

They will celebrate your abundant goodness and joyfully sing of your righteousness.

Psalm 145:7

Your Prayer...

Save us and help us with your right hand, that those you love may be delivered.

Psalm 60

...God's Answer

*All mankind will fear; they
will proclaim the works of God and
ponder what he has done.*

Psalm 64:9

Your Prayer...

Hear my prayer, O Lord, listen
to my cry for help.

Psalm 39:12

…God's Answer

The LORD has heard my cry for mercy;
the LORD accepts my prayer.

Psalm 6:9

You can share everything with God
and be confident that he hears.